Life After Death

Life After Death

poems

by Jane Rohrer

Life After Death

Library of Congress Catalog Control Number: 2022930526
International Standard Book Number: 978-0-9991450-1-2
Printed in the United States of America.
Cover design by Office of Development.

**PAINTED
GLASS
PRESS**

109 Carter Road
Goshen, IN 46526
paintedglasspress.com

In memory of Warren

For my two sons,
daughters-in-law,
and three granddaughters

CONTENTS

Note from the Publisher

Twenty years ago, a fresh voice emerged in poetry to very little fanfare. Jane Rohrer's *Life after Death* was issued in 2002 by a selective poetry publisher, Stanley Moss's Sheep Meadow Press, and many of its poems had first appeared in *The American Poetry Review*. But like most poetry volumes from small presses, without a major award or arduous publicity and promotion, it slipped into oblivion. This new edition of *Life After Death* re-presents the original with a new cover and a few slight corrections approved by the author. The poems, like ferns sunk into the swamp of time, have re-emerged shining and hardened into anthracite. They gleam in their compression, uncompromising vision, and integrity.

The occasion for bringing the poems in Jane's book to a new audience is the exhibition "Hearing the Brush: The Paintings and Poetry of Jane and Warren Rohrer" at the Woodmere Art Museum in Chestnut Hill, Pennsylvania, which combines Jane's poems with a selection of her husband Warren Rohrer's paintings. This reissued volume joins Jane's second book, *Acquiring Land*, published in 2021 by Cascadia Press in conjunction with the exhibition "Field Language: The Paintings and Poetry of Jane and Warren Rohrer" at the Palmer Museum of Art. Jane's poems stand on their own, but are particularly illuminating when viewed in tandem with Warren's work. His monumental abstract paintings, shimmering but inscrutable, suggest the being and consciousness that absorbed Jane's passion and provided companionship as they raised a family and lived in places where they could transform their Mennonite farming roots through a modernist aesthetic by building a life that put art at the center.

When I first met Jane in 1976, she was the articulate, formidable wife of an artist. When I discovered her poetry in the mid-1990s, she had become a poet of vision and authority. Between 1977 and 1985, she published eight poems in *The American Poetry*

Review.[1] Meanwhile, having finished my PhD in English at the University of Pennsylvania, I began collecting work for an anthology that has set the course of my own career—*A Cappella: Mennonite Voices in Poetry* (2003). Work on the anthology led me back to Jane's poems and provided a context for recognizing her as one of the three women literary pioneers.[2] Moreover, I was drawn to Jane's work, with its modernist compression, astonished by her ability to find in natural objects the adequate symbols for thought and emotion.

Life after Death is both elegy and *ars poetica*. The unity that is this volume grows out of a life that integrated artistic vision, commitment to relationships, and a response to the beauty of the world. Jane's great love was her husband, Warren, but her poems register her viewpoint as distinct and unique. One senses the passion generated between two people rooted in a deep communion in such poems as "In the Kitchen Before Dinner" and "The Gearshift Poem." But poems such as "Auction" and "In the Studio" gesture toward her husband's visual imagination through the difference of her own lens. The poet's palette of images is informed by her rural Virginia Mennonite upbringing and family eccentricities—her father's pride in his horses, her mother's compensatory strictness. Living on a farm with Warren for twenty years—although they were not farmers—Jane absorbed the lessons of her past in a setting that emphasized beauty. These places inform the interior landscapes of her imagination. But theirs was not a parochial existence; Warren taught at the University of the Arts and Jane met regularly with a group of poets in Lancaster. They were able to travel and broaden their sense of landscape and place when a group of Lancaster business owners raised enough money for Warren to take a year off from teaching in the early in the early 1970s and travel through Europe with Jane for seven weeks, an experience that pro-

[1] *A Cappella: Mennonite Voices in Poetry* (Univ. of Iowa Press, 2003) 9, 177.

[2] "Three Mennonite Women Poets and the Beginning of Mennonite Poetry in the US: Anna Ruth Ediger Baehr, Jane Rohrer, Jean Janzen." *The Mennonite Quarterly Review* (October 2003) 77.4, 521-546.

foundly affected each of their work. A section of *Life After Death* includes travel poems, some referring to travel with Warren, and some to travel after his death.

After Warren was diagnosed with leukemia in 1978, the Rohrers moved to Philadelphia and sold the farm, purchasing an historic artistic home in Chestnut Hill, the studio of artist Violet Oakley and Edith Emerson, on the edge of Fairmount Park. Warren died in 1995, and for several years Jane devoted herself to the legacy of his work, represented by the Locks Gallery in Philadelphia, and a retrospective exhibit held at the Philadelphia Museum of Art. She also continued to write poetry and travel with her brother Charles. Meanwhile, her mentor Stephen Berg submitted a collection of Jane's poems to Stanley Moss to be considered for book publication.[3] The result was *Life After Death.* As such, this book offers the legacy of a life lived with artistic integrity and vision in communion with another visionary artist, informed by acts of deep attention.

This new edition of *Life After Death* would not exist without the passion and dedication of poet Julia Spicher Kasdorf, whose work on behalf of Warren and Jane's work was instrumental in initiating two exhibitions of their work and a spectacular illustrated catalog and collection of critical essays, *Field Language: The Painting and Poetry of Warren and Jane Rohrer*, edited by Kasdorf along with Christopher Reed and Joyce Henri Robinson, and published by the Palmer Museum of Art at the Pennsylvania State University in conjunction with the exhibition of that title. Philip Ruth translated the old manuscript into its new format, and the Office of Development designed the cover. We wish to thank Sheep Meadow Press for releasing the copyright.

— Ann Hostetler

[3] Julia Spicher Kasdorf, "Coming Back: The Poetry and Life of Jane Rohrer." *Journal of Mennonite Studies* (2018) 36, 43-55.

APPLE

If men are trees
with hanging, hanging fruit
he is the complete orchard:
Smokehouse, Stayman,
Stark, Delicious.

I go out of my body
for his golden apples,
green, ripe, fallen.

SLOWED SUNDAY IN JULY

Sudden, the withering in the pasture,
seeming fallow, the field to the east,
too deep the furrows,
too low the sky.

My mind behaves as though in church,
a child seen but not heard,
listening to an old sermon.

I let my face run down;
it tells the approximate time.
I am waiting
for a miracle or an emergency.

TIME WARP

A cool civilized day
that I have made behave
stretches flat and smooth
and I on top of it.
I drive my horsepower
I choose my numbered routes
cross country, cross roads.
Suddenly, one cross too many
I've crossed some line.
Ahead, behind, black buggies
creak in rhyme.
They move as toys
wound up and set upon the one lane road
and go where they have always gone.
Here I am strange,
highpowered but horseless now,
all my pretty choices
locked in step
between the corn rows and the cows.
So this is how it was—
this creeping trot, this narrow way
from Bird-in-Hand to Paradise?*

*two towns in Lancaster County

FARM IN MY MIND

Most of the time
they stay in the lower field.
I hear their voices,
intermittent,
like bulletins
issued from the radio.
Once my mother came near my house
and on a table spread the objects of her life,
flowers dried
and taken from old books.
Quiet and bending over
she gestured unrecognizably.

Most of the time
I live in an upper field.
The sun shines
warm as approval.
Rain baptizes the shingles,
and what the people do, they do.
Noise comes out
in rounded ohs, *hello, hello*,
children laugh from high in the orchard,
they go away
but send their voices back.
Everywhere is the upper field.

MENNONITE FUNERAL IN THE SHENANDOAH VALLEY

Train up a child
in the way he should go
and when he is old
he will not depart from it.
Proverbs 22: 6

I could never reach this place
but for a memory of Christmas that plays
at the edge of the winter in my mind.

Beside me in the long hallway my father chokes softly.
He is down, now, from the black horse
and back from the worldly track he rode
in widening circles away from her.
In the front parlor she has drawn her circle around her.
Still and unreachable, she receives the favored.
"So nice of you to come."

Outside, on the curved driveway,
we must all fit somehow on this natural occasion.
My aunts, her secular sisters, sit in black cars
smoothing on their gloves
finger by inspected finger.
In the way of things I wait with him
in some other black car
until the column uncouples,
a wake behind her bell-coach inching ahead.

Soundless we creep,
we crawl to the last place
and couple obedient in line
under the old pines
that sigh as in memory.

More of her people wait. *"So nice of you to come."*
I watch her gain the plain doorway, that eye of needle,
and move regally up the gray aisle,
under pink roses,
without her crutch.
We wait in a room strangled of air
and listen to the clock choke.
Mustiness lingers in odor of pamphlet and Sunday vest.
The light, unstained, lies in blocks on the cold floor.
We, the uneven hem of her earthly garment,
are pleated to fit the short front pew.
Breath. I cannot breathe this death.
I hear the varnished pulpit say, "Dearly Beloved,
and you who have left the faith, and this saint."
Her pink fragrance is paling now
and this is bitter bread, O day in my sweet life.
"Goin home
          Goin home."
I take my place with the unforgiven,
see her folded into that satin cathedral.
O Strange return
O train up a child
O child.

SEASONS

Summer hay heads
shrink in heat,
August, bright,
too bright and dying light,
shifts my shadow Bible black.
My shadow slants, not I.

Fall leans into the gap
between my worlds.
One pheasant call
rips the valley seam.
O damn, the whole year
tilts into that fault
on which I do riot choose to think.

I survive the winter
of no mercy,
I do not lie down,
nor sleep,
till Thursday
Maundy Thursday

POEMS COME BACK IN A BLIZZARD
(A Melodrama)

I am the center of the universe;
every flake adjusts its descent
to find me climbing this hill
to the mailbox.
I could be the last Pennsylvania Indian
fighting the wind, or a rural cliché
reaching out to collect
what the world has written me.
This is what the world has written,
"Thanks for writing...
We regret that..."
So even as the forecast was for snow
days ago
an editor sat red and swollen
with blood sucked
from the rejects stiffening
in my hand.

I do not notice dropping
in the snow the pale translucent sheets
of my own skin.
Blowing white coverlets
have done in the path,
are working the hill.
The words are muffle, choke and smother
and I am down
so close to home.

DAILY LIFE

Then, (realizing I had not swung in the hammock
all summer,
that it was rotten from holding rain,
and seeing him mow upside down around the egg-
plant-color pond until he moved
to this side where I could not see him
until he came back up the hill in the green
avenue he had made, to the woodchop pile
of trees felled on the hillside
and, oh, yes, the alfalfa's been cut again
and raked into windrows
with the odor of curing still in the air
from the last crop that lately lay in swaths,)

Is all a day-lily knows.

GARDEN

For years in my garden
I was keeping them alive.
I could feel the drag on the hoe;
it was more than natural toil.
Old asparagus demanded daily attention
and, if neglected on a warm moist day
shot spindly on a stalk
of not much use to anyone.
I noticed over the years
he was easier after the cutting season,
growing to fern in October,
dew and cobwebs glowed on him in the morning,
gray-green, pale, obscured by mist
rising from the valley.
Would he had committed no sin more original
than multiplying here in my private garden.

I make no mistake about my mother.
She was the whole rest of my garden.
Like new lettuce, fragile as tissue
of the thin clear color used to wrap
presents for birthdays, she wilted,
even in spring, if thinned in full sun.

But human beings are meant to be hardy!

A mean rain in summer

washed soil from the roots of poppies,
fluttering fragile ladies' hats
dipping and nodding in the breeze of a garden party.
She leaned. I propped her up with a stone.
Her petals fell in one day.
Death had already taken her. Fumbler.

Lately the notion of freedom
finds some high window
left open to the sun, slips in
like Camus' white dove of a new idea
that is so quiet,
has been there so long, unnamed,
the recognition of it enraptures.

What I cultivate is lettuce.

"THE SUN HAS LEFT THE SKY, OLD MAN"

from the song by Randy Newman

Walking the farm in sunshine
I think I see it whole:
There is the orchard.
I see the pond of origins.
Lower pasture. (In my mind my mother, dead, is there)
Upper field. Garden.
House. I am the house,
my man is in the house,
my man is the house,
I am in the house
and I, Me, Mine, sing the Beatles.

Between the house and the barn
I feel an icy blast that shakes the arrangement.
I must find a place for him
in this metaphor. I remember:
it is May and he is riding a white horse
beside my mother on her favorite white horse
and we children run along after them
on this mystifying evening
when he says, with an arcing gesture,
*"The world will end soon
and all this will be gone."*

From that day on I waited
for the big breaking up of the world.

Last week my father gave me a photograph:
he is nine
his face is smeared by deprivation
his arms are too small for his hands
his hands are too small
for the basket of potatoes.
Whoever held the camera
was interested in potatoes.
I'm reading the back of the picture,
"Keep in family. Remember."
I could let him be that large maple
below the barn,
trying to reach heaven after sundown.

God, he is out too far
on the limb of himself, carrying potatoes.

James Wright was wrong about the branch not breaking.

MAKING HAY

Things come into focus during the afternoon
as I stand behind the large painting,
holding the brace steady
against a playful wind.
I hear the camera click
as he photographs the whole picture
then walks up close
and details converging rows of color.
We are on a broad flat place
near the barn
in light haze,
ideal for photographing
and for making hay.
I see John enter the alfalfa field
with a six mule team.
pulling a gasoline engine and a bulky baler
to begin working the windrows,
the whole contrivance crossing the field
in the lock-step rhythm
of an old poem.
The first bale hangs at the top of the chute;
John's son pulls it down
and stacks it at the back of the wagon.
The little girl tugs at it, also.
Her dress is the purple of the painting's edge
where the hay-green dissolves.

I am thinking of cows
in winter, chewing,
and of the idea of the cud.

TAKING OFF

I write to contain the panic,
telling myself this plane is going nowhere,
that it's not a plane at all
but the lobby of the Pittsburgh Hilton,
but writing brings the familiar panic
attached to blank paper
and available pencils.

Of course, you cannot necessarily
govern an engine for long.
Inevitably we move,
riding the bumps of earth
to the imperceptible lift
and it is as though I've chosen
times of my life for the trip,
that unfurl from the jet's sleek tail
banner-like.
I cannot see them but I know they are there.

Now I become wild in the mind
thinking I've outwitted encumbrance
and can fly on,
never to return
to the smoothed meadow,
domesticated snakes indolent on rocks
in the watercress stream.
I inhale the illusion of freedom.

I cannot see them but I know they are there,
the not quite dead
burying the dead,
short-sheeted in shallow graves.

PHOTOGRAPH IN THE MAIL

So there you are—
planted on the rocks at Marblehead
hair caught, wind-sculpted, in gray rock sky.
What face,
what handsmoothed
          hand-traced face
that taunts a gray rock ocean.
I could get lost on the continent in your look.

Nineteen, where have you gone?
One, two, three years
I could hold in my pocket
and six I found one day in the barn,
but nine—for your little nine clues
I searched all over the farm.
And now you have discovered America.
Nineteen speeds straight,
interstate, to twenty-one.

I think you must have driven
to the other side of black
in the green Mustang.

I say you won't be back.

ZEN POEM

I am here in the highest story of my house
looking out for the snowplow.
We've been snowed-in for days
and one priority has superseded
an entire list: to move about in the world.
Look at the pond.
It has a matte surface, gray.
The snow melted in before it froze solid
and then sleet coated it.
It's the sleet that hobbles the plows.

Friends grow wise in the city.
They call and say the country must be beautiful.
It is beautiful. As far as the eye can see
it is beautiful.
Nothing crosses her despotic beauty.

I go down where it is warm.
I say, *"One is always bound;*
if not by snow, accumulations."
He says, *"Don't get philosophical,"*
hands me a shovel and says, *"Shovel."*
We go out where it is cold
and shovel.

IN THE KITCHEN BEFORE DINNER

The winter sky past the feeder,
beyond the wood of straight trees
and the field rising to the ridge,
is unnervingly delicate.
But you are acquainted with the country
and you know poems. You've heard this.

Years, years and years, I've looked out
from this window, stirring—
straight out of the sun
a cardinal swoops to the feeder,
his sweep, not his shape,
the unstrokable wing of art.
Seeing that,
I want to tell you:
the sun of poems is on the snow
on the slope past the wood
to the pond. What I see at five o'clock.
It marries the music from my living room.
It is not that simple.
I cannot explain it.
Saying that,
I think I cannot ever leave.
I'm grounded by attachment,
I'm rapacious for facts:
That bowl.
His gloves on the chair, holding each other.
These I can explain.

THE GEARSHIFT POEM

If I look at his hand on the gearshift
my thighs will open
my palm will settle to his thick wrist
feel which way to move
down the back of his hand to the skin tip
up his sleeve to rough
jacket shoulder shirt neck hair black bouncing
to my hand sending
messages to my whole self here in the
car after twenty-
eight years it is still happening
if his hand ever,
now gliding level first to window
then to radio,
lights I will stroke it thinking yes
and wanting not to cage him in habit.

ORCHARD IN THE SPRING

I am shaking like a leaf in the orchard.
Green parachutes are caught in the trees;
a lace drapes the crabapple.
On the ground thick pruned branches
lie in disarray, waiting.
I am not waiting.
If you are calling me,
I am over here, staring at the ground
where fallen cuttings meet and pass
and a short-lived face appears
as a shadow on the blowing grass.

I am sad in the white drizzle of blossoms.
Elmer, in the lower field,
bobs along atop the plow
drawn by a six-mule team
opening a furrow, closing it,
opening, closing, the livelong day.

I lie down in the grass and look up.
Now I am waiting.
Someone I know is that dried apple
holding on since last fall.
Soon a green shoot will push it from the limb
to the ground.

READING AT BREAKFAST

"So possible green the spring,
so green the farm I thought we'd leave."
He reaches for his cup
and I touch his hand, *"More coffee?"*
He looks up from his stack of papers,
The Sunday Times,
an art book, blankfaced.
The art book says the last painting's been painted,
says this yellow quiet corner
tilts above a final abyss
even while the bottles on the sill,
the nasturtiums and the thyme
are the same
and I see his face change:
They come still
down the long lane of his mind,
dumb things,
crude images in drifting light
shuffling toward the surface,
dazzling, awkward, oblivious.

UNDER ANESTHETIC

I do not want to leave.
I go up slowly, my bed following.
I float under acoustical tile,
actors pass by on the high television,
nurses converge beneath me,
gliding without legs.
Hanging there,
I do not think of God at all,
Parents, sisters, brothers, hardly,
I fight to hold on to my sons.
I lose them just after my daughters-in-law.
I am beyond marriage,
can no longer feel his hand.
Then everything goes;
I belong to them.

Floating down,
limbs attach trunk,
neat assemblage on the efficient horizon.
I lift a heavy finger, panic.
My roots. I panic for my roots.
I wait. Nothing happens.
They've folded my mind with my belongings.
This is a body place.

I look for but never find
that which was lost.

Back home, waiting for leaves to grow,
The waiting screws my thumbs to the wall.

THE TRIP

I just came home from shopping in the town.
One street was roped off for a funeral.
"She was nineteen,"
they said of the girl in the box;
I am thinking of matrons in tennis socks
when my telephone rings
and the matron says,
"I had the most MARVelous trip to Nepal
where no one kills a flea
including those in my bed,
or the rat in my room in Katmandu."

GOING TO KERKYRA

Now, years later, it is here in my mind
suspended, floating on the mirror sea
like that floating rock far out
eye-level, off the cliff
by the white-arched monastery
Paleocastritsa.

Behind that woman there
in the vineyard high above Ay Gordis
A red sun slides toward a purple sea.
She balances it on her shoulder
effortlessly as she works and sings,
sings and piles her donkey higher than herself,
beasts of burden, both,
she with outstretched purple hands,
going on home through the poppies.
Below that sheer sharp drop
the Ionian crashes against the rocks,
piles up white shapes
of cathedrals crumpled on their sides.

Kerkkyra, I hear your men sing,
your sheep bells sprinkle the distance
with a thin musical rain, and the sheep,
aimless in low cloud cover,
wander up the stony face
of Pantocrator.

Let me tell you about coming home,
about how finally gray my barn is
and about not going back.

CORFU PHOTOGRAPH

Now that I see it again
I believe it:
The lamb is waiting, tied to the downspout
on the sidewalk
by a house in Corfu town
Easter Saturday.
The red ribbon around his neck
blows in spring air
and the little lamb tail
flicks upward against the stucco,
fur-like below the window
whose shutters are tied
so they will not slam.
There is a doorway on the right
and steps.

He is at least the lamb of god,
long gone now
except for the slit of his throat
bleeding in my mind.

OTHER WOMEN

Tonight I cannot sleep.
I see her at a window
as I saw her the day before Easter,
in Greece,
at a window high above the street.
She is cradling an empty waterpot,
her vessel of sacrifice.
"Why don't you go ahead and throw it out?"
a man beside me yells.
Throw it out
comes back to me now,
held in my throat like my voice.
She throw, throw, throws it out
and the explosion
blasts her back into the darkened room.

Other times when I'm awake,
other women
unfilled or emptied
or with a flaw,
one I was born to, or was,
was thinking of, or saw,
sit on my high sill.
Vessels of sacrifice and dispensation,
these urns, these vases wait,
all mouth and bottomless.

I am unaccustomed to the breakage of women,
breakage of women
breakage of women.
I feel shards sharp under my feet
on the streets of the world.

ELENA, LAST NUN OF SANTA MARIA, CORFU

A relic shawled in black
mourned all the others, dead.
As one who kept a vigil
by the door of a dying parent
she existed, resided, even,
beside the archaic church
on the acropolis of the island,
at home within the perimeter
of a mere umbrella
when fine rains blew down from Italy.

All that month I walked the Analypsis Road
from Mon Repos.
In relentless light
I skirted the olive groves
at the edge of the old sea
and tried to read the mainland.
Each day Elena presided at the table
under the lemon tree
and I was prisoner to the ceremony:
Turkish coffee
boiled up three times
over diminished fire,
offered properly Greek
in small cup with tiny spoon,
with thin curl of lemon peel
and cold water,

a glass in whose name.
Some days it took longer than possible;
she seemed bound to her task
by such fragile remembrance.

I never understood the conspiracy between us
until now. She was Greece,
Colossus fallen,
and all of us
with our coffee cups remain
without our mother
out in the rain.

AUCTION

The day is drizzly, I am gloomy
here with you at this gathering
of your side of the family.
I watch you appreciate the occasion
and you are smiling,
watching a movie I haven't seen.
You see benevolently,
are comfortably clothed
in a long warm genealogy
but I am chilly here
and tell you this.
Please talk to me about those old men,
your uncles in great-uncle suits
whose wives are inflated under coats
and have tightly fettered hair.
Why do they tabulate the price
of every leaky bucket
and grieve to part with shovels?
Listen to them bid, calling dollars,
holding up a number against the wind.

Why have we come here?
The heirlooms are gone, long disbursed,
and the acres divided,
plowed under and planted,
and have sprouted into this,
these wart-like houses on the land.

Yet this draws you as to an origin.
I wonder, if we dig straight down
under Uncle Jason, there,
will we come to it?

Look, I'm not buying any of this.
These little final piles of things—
their truth is the truth of funerals.

TRACKING THE AMISH QUILT

(I came on it at the Whitney Museum
In 1972. An art-
fogged curator straying wide afield
discovered it first: Pennsylvania.
Amish. "*Bars.*" Circa 1860.
Amish? Where had I been? My neighbors!
Did Elmer and Lizzie and children,
did bundles of children sleep under
the likes of this brooding blue statement?)

At nine I stop to pick up Lizzie
for the drive to Nine Points where her
mother will show me a quilt for sale.
Waiting, I watch Elmer bend, threading the
rows with seed, covering his straight
design. God. It's now I glimpse another quilt,
ragged beauty thrown out by the barn.
Speak not what might have been. No. What was
and is no more. Lizzie says, *"Oh that*

old thing. You may have it, it's worn out.
What are you looking for?" I hear my
mouth clattering. We drive by fields mute
in the sun and dark floating meadows,
Amish unconscious shapes. Look, I
saw it, also, at a dealer's house.
I could not afford its slow red burn

of stripes across receding brown ground
of intricate stitching, just crib-size.

Think what Amish boy in flat straw hat
dragged it along a brown deep furrow
behind his daddy, what daddy turned
behind his team and saw it only
a quilt, somber and familiar.
The high price of being innocent
is innocence. Conversing of things
we pull up at Lizzie's old homeplace.
Two little girls and one tiny boy

drift down the lawn to the car—Oh, please
do not remind me children should be seen and not heard
—inexpressive, staid
as miniature old folk. Lizzie's
mother, slight and long-necked as a
goose, cranes from the porch, greeting, eyeing
me, anxious for the possible sale
but mindful some time must pass between
meeting, meeting of mind, and money.

You should see this immaculate farm
where Lizzie grew up. Removed from main
roads, it forms a hollow to its hill,
completes itself. How they plant flowers
here, according to authority,
how they love and tend the straight rows of
vegetables forever, naming each
variety, saving its best seed,

replanting endlessly, endlessly.

We hear an unearthly commotion.
A heavy iron machine dragged by six
mules passes on its way to the barn.
Men, animals, machine, make noises.
A daughter-in-law approaches, asks
if we want to buy yesterday's bread.
Where is it, my naïve Rothko quilt,
the beautiful, mysterious quilt
for which I came, for which I loiter?

We move to the new linoleum
kitchen. Lizzie's mother tremblingly
fetches her quilt from a dark side room.
She shows it, unfurls it to my eyes,
holds two corners tightly, shakes it, waits.
A Nine Patch Square. Its center glows old
in a newly-grafted border field,
so informed, so practical, so ugly.
The best cf both worlds. A stitch in time.

Waste not, want not. He who hesitates—

Suppose the small facts of my life
are scattered, that I must look
for them down these side roads
as though they are lambs
forgotten, left
out in the meadow-
mind.

ON THE TURNPIKE

On the turnpike I search for the fare
in the small soft deerskin purse
I've been carrying since we divided her things.
She could not be more daily with me
had she left me money.
This thin pursed pouch reminds me
she owned nothing open-mouthed
even one wild scream.

Small change.
It's all here every nickel and dime of it.
Her first penny, you might say.

PICTURES AT AN EXHIBITION

"I wondered what that red streak was.
It was light bouncing off a pheasant's neck,"
my husband said, putting the binoculars
on the breakfast table by the window.
Imagine that. And imagine a duck
quiet as a decoy
on the unfrozen rim of the pond.
Imagine that deer near the west wood
prancing on her tiny hooves.

Now imagine the west wood,
how it sliced the winter light
and hid the far view,
before they cut it down.
Now I see everything:
far field
and even farther fields:
a long low horse barn
red vertical feeder, my inverted obelisk,
new red gates
red pick-up truck.

My father's gone off
and left his toy horses out again.

A COMPARISON OF HORSES

Friday morning, October, rain.
Those are the facts here at the window.

The drought lasted all summer
but the horses managed.
They ate weeds, ranging the hill,
and came to the pond at twilight
where I saw them silhouetted
against the sliver of white gold
at the horizon.
I kept wondering all summer
why I did not straighten in my chair
and lean forward at the sight,
why even their soft whinny in the night
did not arouse.

Yesterday I drove to the city
and went up the gray stairs
to the gallery.
Why, look at those sculptures
on gray pedestals,
about waist high
if you are a short person.
I was tempted to pet them,
small gray animal forms,
some of them horses
in a seeming random scattering,

grazing into the corners of the room.
Standing there, I was almost nostalgic
for the horses
I had left at home,
but blissfully removed, momentarily,
from the tyranny of the natural.

Today I am back with the horses,
eleven black shapes
in the center of the window.
Now they shift into a line,
their legs a moving fence.

I will go again.

CALLING THE DOGS SOFTLY

She tiptoes in libraries,
does not pirouette on oriental rugs
or sound her horn in a hospital zone.
She places her cup lightly
in the good china saucer,
and when the dogs slip their leashes
she finds them in the dark
calling their names softly.

RETURNING TO THE SCENE

Waiting for my car in the Volkswagen garage
at 8:00 in the morning
I start to imagine my father's funeral.
That docile old man in heavy coat and arctics
conjures him, I suppose.

I have gone as far as the church
at my mother's funeral ten years ago.
The details are clear:
he sits caught
in only the threads on his back,
he makes a small noise
like the complaint
of a wounded animal, trapped.
"Your car," they address my reasonable self, *"is ready."*

When he dies
I will go to the same church
and fold myself into the pew
ribboned off for survivors.
I try to imagine it; *my car is ready—*
The details are unclear: I am eight years old.
He is combing my waistlength hair.

THE ONLY WOMAN PSYCHIATRIST

The only woman psychiatrist of my acquaintance
was born Amish, and growing up, feared going blind
reading forbidden books with a flashlight,
beneath the covers
of her Amish bed.

The only woman psychiatrist of my acquaintance
gave up her practice saying, *"psychiatrists are crazy,"*
and moved to Florida to run a motel.

The only woman psychiatrist turned motel proprietor
of my acquaintance
gave up her motel because, *"people are crazy,"*
and moved into a motor home
to look for the perfect place.

Dear Ruth: I do not want to ride fat and homeless
in your Winnebago.
I want to walk into my living room
and lift a glass in candlelight
to an intimate group
of the crazies you left behind.

LANDING IN A NEW PLACE

St. Maarten is clean of me,
I have not written on it.
After three days
I try to read what's going on.
I watch a chameleon,
worrying he is a cockatrice,
bisect a crack in the concrete apron
of the pool, there by my brother,
young, finishing a fifth
at ten in the morning.
He is the fatigue I feel
even when absent from him
in my reasonable life,
he is what I see now
when I hold this paper between me and the ocean.
My husband, out far past a coco palm,
facing away to South America
from a reef of honeycomb coral,
is like a mirage.
Now I make him disappear.
I make of this paper
a funnel, a vortex,
to spin my brother clean and dry,
I write, *"it is written,"* while he drinks.

When I come here again,
breathe out, breathe in,

he will be dead,
my failure the fly floating in his glass half-empty.

ARTISTS' WORKSHOP

Turnpikes converge and become a road,
the road narrows to a trail
and the trail widens
to a clearing near a lake.
There are signs everywhere on the trees:
Be Creative   *Do Not Encourage Bears*

The north woods is green-black,
full of fur and noise and eye-gleams
close together in the night.
In the day
the lake is not a simple water;
I have seen it glint mean
against the muzzle of the island
thrusting into it.

The task is
to row across that lake
to the ocean somewhere
and never look back.
Say, lovely blue heron,
will you go with me,
have you ever been
there?

Bear, bear
give me your fur
and your fat for the winter
and your little pig eyes that
scare people

Time is short.

We spent so much of it getting here.
I hear voices, the woods
and those of the artists;
some days I listen, some I talk.
There is hiding among the trees,
there is restlessness on the shore.
Lights burn all night in studios,
all night in cabins.
People toast each other
and talk of other worlds:
"I loved it there"   *"I wonder what it will be like."*

Nobody is allowed to stay here forever.
When it is over we all go
to an individual place,
the makers of boats,
the users
and those who nibbled trees
with their front teeth.

ARTISTS' WORKSHOP 2

I am struck by what I see
from my cabin: a squirrel,
the blue university truck
unloading at the kitchen,
something fluffy sifting
from the trees or sky.
Through the lower right window pane
just to the left of the paper towels
the famous guest-artist's belly protrudes.
He's leaning against the dining hall
waiting for dinner.
Richard says he is subversive,
photographed in airports,
tailed in lobbies.
Here he has painted the girls from Baltimore
and the girls from Saskatoon.
Soon he will go to Las Vegas
on an important project.

DEAR DUANE HANSON,

I first saw your sculpture
at the Pennsylvania Academy of the Fine Arts
in Philadelphia.
Your *Man with Beer Can* was nearly arrested
for loitering; they thought he was asleep
but he was merely plastic.
A long time ago, in Philadelphia,
Gordon Bailey Washburn said
art has vitality
and vitality
is the difference
between a sleeping cat and a dead cat.

Crossing the country last summer
I saw your models everywhere:
in a Badlands heat wave
sightseeing in air conditioned cars
that kept their waxy faces from melting,
waiting for you in North Dakota
she sat dazed by the devil wind,
the screeching of the windmills
and bald creatures crawling up from gopher holes.
They rode, they stood, they wait
in Howard Johnsons Anywhere.

Now here I see your work again
in the Nelson Gallery in Kansas City,

wearing Hawaiian shirts
and sitting in mesh chairs
in plots of a size reminiscent
of the front yards of RVs.
Nearby, a guard wears a small tag,
I am not a work of art.

I am remembering an ancient celedon bowl
in the Cleveland Museum, where,
Duane, Duane, the morning light streamed down again.

WHEN IT WAS TIME

If you sat on a high porch
when it was time
and magnolia blossoms began to fall
from the tall tree
seemingly timed
but actually in random sequence
not spiraling or fluttering
but dropping silent, plumb
you might think The Concert Singer
by Eakins,
in gown maybe pink but seeming white,
with her mouth open, pear-shaped,
had dropped her handkerchief
and it was drifting silent, plumb
to her hem and satin toes
as she inaudibly sighs
to the petal-white back
of her hand.

I WISH I MIGHT HAVE SEEN

I wish I might have seen
that pheasant-cock stalk
just now past the window,
among clumps of daffodils
under the firethorn bush,
on his way to the back pasture
and the mayapples spreading there.
I saw nothing.
A pheasant in the mind, perhaps,
fixed there late last fall
when expectation widened the eye.

Cockbird in spring,
show me again.

SMART POETRY

Smart poetry, I conclude, closing the anthology.
Smart young men in universities
wrote about the world in terms of their penises
in the sexual sixties.
Genitals in poems
are not news
anymore.

Nature is far away.
I walk down 4th and pause at Kater;
That sign,
S. Dorfman Elastic Hose Trusses
has already entered literature.
Find a sign so at odds
with a city in renaissance
(Elastic Hose Penises Trusses)
And you've found a found poem.

I'm confused crossing Bainbridge
about the wellsprings of poetry.
It is spring.
I practice acquainting my ear with the despotic beauty of noise.

SITTING BY THE WINDOW

I must garner my courage
against a time I need it,
not scatter it like candy corn
to the chickens of habit.
Deer, at the edge of easy vision,
cavort on the granite-hard
winterfield.

But should my world invert,
my mind be forced to scavenge
in some old chickenhouse
where news comes relayed
as by telephone
and suffering rings obscenely,
should death, that old cliché,
offend us ...

Then the courage I have hoarded
will shape itself
and lie with me
like a lover.

CHARLIE, NO CITY DOG

Prowls so primitively.
What grotesque
what colossal bones
what mule shank dragged
from the railroad gorge.
There, stand human-like, by the tree
and I will photograph and caption you,
Charlie, With Bone of Amish Mule or Cow.

Other nights he digs ancestors
from the woods behind the house,
unguessable parts,
bone of whose bone?

DOG TWO

Something white comes out of the dark wood.
It's Charlie. He's been digging up my
ancestors again. I hear I could
join them, anytime, in a bone dry

grave. Charlie doesn't know which are his
bones or theirs except theirs lie docile
in mathematical rows, nothing amiss.
What elegant system, the fossil.

I'm loafing these days on my high porch,
an uneasy place to pass my life.
This view of the wood. Often I watch
them congregate. This husband, that wife.

So you're going on back, are you, Charles,
scraping your belly on the wire fence.
Old father metaphor, my quarrels with you
my private recompense.

Tell them I've been hijacked, set down
in Firenze where I'm eating fungi porcini.
Tell them I'm drinking Antinori. I buried
them in a dark café last Monday.

FLYING IN A SMALL PLANE

When I climb to another atmosphere
in a big plane, I am born again.
We are just practicing.
We hang in the slippery air,
our small engines teasing
the pull of the earth.
The doctors in the cockpit
take it up to eight thousand feet
and level, chatting into the radio.
From the passenger's seat I watch them play.
It is not a serious trip.

Dying, she said from within me,
is like flying in a small plane.

COMMUNION

I need your hands to speak
the parts of my body
until they know their names.

(When I was young and went away from home
they used to say, *"Remember who you are."*
But how could I remember
what I had never known?)

I need your thighs.
I need you to come into me
for I am lonely in my room
and without you I am
a pewful of women
all knuckles and knees
hearing this is my body,
this do in remembrance of me.

IN THE STUDIO

He is brushing
stroke by rose madder stroke
on the clean ground
of the canvas.
The documentary filmmaker leans close,
his big camera
obscuring his head.
The local newspaper photographer
leans into the space
behind the filmmaker,
adjusts his lens
and photographs the filmmaker
filming the artist painting.
I am a camera.
This is your picture
of what I see.
Now you are in the picture
And behind you stands one
who sees the whole thing.
and behind him …
and behind him …
his ear close, hearing the brush.

BAD TRUTH

If I had no memory
I would say this is perfect,
this June late afternoon
and early evening.
Cat is walking the rim of the pond below
and here on the terrace
we drink some wine while dinner cooks.

Let me go on:
we're eased in green and purple canvas chairs;
behind us
through the blue screen door
hard rock rolls rumors
which turn explicit as I write.

He is reading North of Jamaica
as a bird of classical proportion
flies between us to the walnut tree
and I am holding *History of My Heart* by Pinsky
when this day tilts
on a Rickenbacker rip, a drum-thump
and a bass full of moans
for a bad truth.

The garden hose lies coiled and reminds me,
yesterday I saw a snake in the gully
turn its dry white underbelly up.

THE WHITE BALLOON

Up against the stone wall of my old white house,
snowed blind by light on the white laurel blossoms
drifting onto the terrace
and covering my feet slowly,
I achieve lack of focus.
Listen. I turned the volume high and his voice
rolls through the blue door, *"Come on, babe, follow me,*
I'm the Pied Piper," rides high on guitars
pouring it all over me and the pale petals.

Last week after a graduation, from a knoll
in the court of brick and ivy,
someone suddenly hugged me,
and I looked up and over the caps and gowns
and parents eating reception strawberries
and there was a white balloon
just clearing the tallest building I could see.
From clusters tied to the handrail of the steps
for the recessional from the Academy of Music
one slipped away . . .

I have played this tape twelve or thirteen times today
and am quite untied, remembering the white balloon,
which as this pied voice is *come on babe*
and how can I, considering the blossoms?

SEEING THINGS

I can see
that pretty girl swinging along down there
with her hair floating
as a dark cloud.
She's under the chestnut tree
and chestnuts are falling;
they hit the pavement around her,
burst, scattering across the street
between us. Why,
I have never seen this before.
Not quite like this. And
look, she's my daughter-in-law
coming from her house, in restoration,
to mine, restored.

METAPHOR

Years ago in a writing class
the professor talked about a poet
who lost his mind
trying to decide
whether to live in the city
or the country.

Twenty years I lived on that farm
for the look of the orchard and the fields
in mist, in rain, in snow,
and, most of all, in blossom,
until, in loneliness,
one day I left it
and began to long for it
like everybody else.

The other day at a party
I heard a single word
fall toward me through the talk of friends
like a tree uprooted,
crashing through new green growth.
Was it orchard?
Was it pond,
or simply hill?

NEIL AND THE FIELD

for Doris

We call it Warren's field,
his borrowed acres that evoke the fields
he paints here in his studio
an hour from there.
The light is the same.
It drifts across in pattern
minimal as those antique Amish quilts
we see m museums.
The landscape seems to kneel
toward the headwaters of the Conestoga.
I doubt the farmer knows his fields better
except by the seat of his pants
as he contours the slopes up to and around
the white Mennonite church near Churchtown.
It's usually closed. Such old bones.

Mennonite farmers cultivated the field, or it lay fallow,
for hundreds of years.
Meanwhile, in the great northwest,
Neil cultivated himself in privilege
in the shadow of Mt. Hood,
his touchstone, he always said.
His seasons produced a beauteous brood of Botticellis,
lined up for the parade
when Daddy boogied by on booze.
The parade closed down
when the Buddha said to Neil,

"Go east, young man, go east,
it's a movable Mt. Hood!"
Packing up his Eastern feast
he moved it all the way to Philadelphia.

One day the four of us drove out to the field.

When Neil was half out of his mind
with what was gumming up the machinery of his cells,
the Lama spoke of death.
Neil swung wild as a possessed pendulum
from aw fuck it!
to the preternatural pellucidity of,
"Scatter me in Warren's field."

There is the bardo that is and the bardo that will be,
out here in the wind
where the three of us make a funeral without tomb.
Furtive, clandestine,
just out of view of neighboring farmhouses,
we gloss a new ritual upon an ancient order.
So small in the distant curve of furrow,
she comes toward us whispering mantras,
weeping as she sows.
I see Millet, I see Van Gogh.
Ashes and bits of bone rise on the wind
like a figure in smoke.
The genie is out of the jar.
I can't stuff it back.
A wild voice gusts in my throat,

"Oh, plume of Neil, fly. Don't lie in Warren's field."

Soon it snowed.
Just before spring plowing,
they spread manure on the field.

ROOM 703

I see now you were rehearsing death
that day at the University of Pennsylvania Hospital.
I thought it was just a continuation
of our 46 year conversation
and that, since you could no longer paint,
you had turned poet.

You spoke from a vast white prairie of bed,
a place with no direction:
"It's Mr. Alexander."
"Who is Mr. Alexander?" I asked.
You answered, *"This thing inside me.*
He's a gnome-like creature with a large head.
We are co-owners of an ocean-going vessel."

When I opened the curtains and windows
to the clear space above the city,
again you spoke, as though saying something important,
"You know that saying, between a rock and a hard place?
Well, it should be put in a box on a high shelf
and brought out only for an occasion like this."

My end of the conversation hung in my throat.
Some hard place.
We could simply wait for Mr. Alexander
to come in his vessel
or we could go out on intravenous tubes.

And what did I mean, we?

For the third year
on the day of his death
I left my house on a hopeful journey
to Rhoads Pavilion
and the purr of an elevator
large and posh enough to move into.
There I was again, a visitor.

I walked straight ahead
past the closed door of Room 703,
past the nurses station
lest someone say, *"May I help you?"*
and I answer, *"Where have you put him?"*

HOTEL

You have been gone for years
yet I live with you.
Nights are best
because of the dreams,
bridging as they do
the dimensions
of this three-dimensional chess board
we move upon.

Take the night we met
in the hotel of before and after.
It was almost too far for you to come
but you were happy
and had a message.
I see my hand click the lock
and hear the click
and say, *"We haven't a moment to lose."*

And we dance.
We danced a dance we had never learned,
coming as we did from people
who applied themselves diligently
to the practice of refraining from dance.
Anyway, I will never forget it.
Once we got the hang of it,
it was way beyond anything
from our loveliest days, don't you think?

Even so,
so insubstantial was its perfection,
the old flawed days haunt
and the memory of material mesmerizes.
I say bodybody.

DREAM

Last night I dreamed a mythical cathedral
for a celebration memorial for Jennie.
I chose a gown and then chose again
before presenting myself to the occasion,
this gift to Dan and his family.
The music was Mahler
and it was so overwhelming
as to summon my husband, also,
from his dwelling in my dreams
and then, sure enough,
the boys said, with all the octane of *Elvis is in the building,*
that he had arrived
and was down the nave to the left.
I made my way toward him,
and he was wearing, as we say here,
Armani Black Label.
But it was far beyond that.
The robing was sublime,
of, perhaps linen,
tailored with fine detail
that translated the joy
in his muscular earthly gait
and outheld human arms.

Here I claimed an of-this-world exclusivity
and gave up my body
to the curve below his shoulder
which had always been my home.

FIELDS IN SNOW

You have obviously been here
since my last visit
and I like what you've done.
But, is it landscape
or is it art?
It's all so confusing
with you coming from the other side.

Calligraphy, there on the contours of the field,
scribbling in stalks and stacks
left from the fall,
is visible in the distant upper levels
of the canvas.
if it is a canvas.
But, it's the wash of thin white,
just a sift of snow,
or is it white,
that erases the visual samsara
and beckons me to you beyond the pale.

We've been split like a schist.
Here I am and there you are,
parallel.

SAIL AWAY

Can't stop walking
these gleaming decks
into and out of
the music aft.
It's a Charles Ives minute.

In any direction
nothing but horizon
or no horizon
sea and sky all the same;
turn me upside down
no top no bottom
inside a pale gray
silken sphere.
Dolphins in ballet off the bow—
no instinctive animal thrashing about
but a concerted offering of beauty.
We have no place to sleep
but this sweet swell.

After dinner
I take my coffee
all the way up
in the dark.
There against the black velvet,
visible for a moment
when the ship's reflected light

outlines the shape of their breasts
and long tumescent necks,
geese in formation.

We must be near land.

I want to go home.

THE CONSOLATION OF CATHEDRALS

The Cathedral of Milan was closed for a funeral
so we took the elevator to the roof
to look around.
I caught my breath at the city
spread out below
like a lawn of roofs.

Stopped suddenly in my mincing steps
on the precarious skywalk
by a lavish rush of music rising,
I fit my face into a small broken pane on the dome.
So far below as to appear toy-like,
the pieces of the tableau:
The coffin, draped in silk and gravity,
mourner-trailed,
appeared so easily lifted as to be empty.
I saw the performance as a morality play
for us on the dome.
A pale column of frankincense
spiraled genie-like into the vault, and
then the organ, all its stops out,
and the chorus, fullthroated,
released Mozart's Requiem Mass, the Lacrimosa
up and over me and it rose and spread, a protest
against the most sad state,
into the sky.
Even now, remembering,
I steady myself, spread-eagled on the dome.

On the day before Easter Sunday, in Martinique,
from the narrow street by Eiffel's cathedral
where I stood shaking my head in disbelief
at that gothic beauty constructed of cast iron plates,
in a tropical country I heard a soprano
begin rehearsal:
her voice, floating above a muted organ
ministering lovingly to Mozart.
"Enfold, enfold," she sang
I waited and it came again, and again,
enfold, enfold,
until up and down the street
people tilted their faces upward
as though in gratitude.

Even now, remembering
I steady myself, enfolded, within.

TOURIST

I sent my griefs out of town
but I see they are back, circling the airport.
I hope to get off the ground
before they are cleared to land.
They are not allowed on this trip.
My hopeful, new stripped-down life is in one bag—
"Check it, please,
Check it all the way through."

POEM

Who are these people here on the deck,
feet planted against the rock and roll of the waves?
Are we on stage in the play of the day?
That man who smiles—does he get it
or is he just playing his part?

I try to take the moment in,
paper to pencil
but nothing comes of the connection.
What goes by goes right by me.
While I am thinking poem
the poem flies up like a released balloon
darting crazily as it deflates.
You know that crude, in-your-face sound
of a balloon losing it.
It drops, a flaccid skin here in my hand,
of no use, without a word to its name
even though one hovered over my page
for a moment, I swear it did,
just grazing my attention.

Even now, someone else is reaching for it.
No doubt.

SMALL MUSEUM

I've built a small museum in memory,
hired myself as curator of expressions
surviving my father's innocent and terrible life
on the Shenandoah mountain, circa 1905.

I see it as a series of small shrines
resembling those erected at hairpin curves
on the road up Mt. Pantocrator, Corfu
where cars had gone off the edge
and people were killed, but,
while those memorials look like Joseph Cornell boxes,
I see these as word art shrines,
Ed Ruscha-like, as in I Don't Want No
                                        Retro
                                        Spective.

My father called one field
the Sunside Field, near the top,
where crops held on as best they could,
and one FAR FIELD.
Then there was RAILROAD FIELD
even though the railroad
was a day's journey by horse,
and KETTLE FIELD.
CASPER OAT PATCH was his uncle.
When I close my eyes now,
I see COLOR FIELD.

A mountain man driving a manure spreader
broke a spoke in his wheel
and fixed it with a stick,
leaving SPREADER STICK in our talk.
In the woods on the trails
between cabins of the clan
are spots spoken of as DEER LICK
and SALT LICK.

VALENTINE

I will make you a valentine of snow;
you can let it melt
and dip your fingers in
to know how a rivulet felt.

Or lift it to your lips
to slake a thirst—
if you remember sips
and thirst and lips.

Where you have gone, or go
I will send you a valentine of snow
in case you do not touch snow, now.

CPSIA information can be obtained
at www.ICGtesting.com
Printed in the USA
BVHW040108270422
635176BV00006B/46